# 'GREEKS' AND 'GREECE' IN MESOPOTAMIAN AND PERSIAN PERSPECTIVES

# THE TWENTY-FIRST
# J. L. MYRES MEMORIAL LECTURE

## 'GREEKS' AND 'GREECE'
## IN
## MESOPOTAMIAN AND PERSIAN
## PERSPECTIVES

A Lecture delivered at

New College, Oxford, on 7th May, 2001

by

## AMÉLIE KUHRT

LEOPARD'S HEAD PRESS

2002

Published in 2002 by
LEOPARD'S HEAD PRESS LIMITED
1–5 Broad Street, Oxford OX1 3AW

ISBN 0 904920 44 5

*The Committee wishes to express its warmest thanks to the Marc Fitch Fund for a generous grant towards publication.*

Typeset by Denham House, Yapton, West Sussex
and printed in Great Britain

# ABBREVIATIONS

| | |
|---|---|
| *ABC* | A. K. Grayson, *Assyrian and Babylonian Chronicles* (Texts from Cuneiform Sources 5), Locust Valley, N.Y., 1975 |
| *AchHist VI* | *Achaemenid History VI: old cultures in a new empire*, ed. by H. Sancisi-Weerdenburg and A. Kuhrt, Leiden, 1991 |
| *AchHist VIII* | *Achaemenid History VIII: continuity and change*, ed. by H. Sancisi-Weerdenburg, A. Kuhrt and M.C. Root, Leiden, 1994 |
| *AfO* | *Archiv für Orientforschung* |
| *AMI* | *Archäologische Mitteilungen aus Iran* |
| *ASNP* | *Annali della Scuola Normale*, Pisa |
| *BASOR* | *Bulletin of the American Schools of Oriental Research* |
| *BCH* | *Bulletin de Correspondance Hellénique* |
| *BHLT* | A. K. Grayson, *Babylonian Historical-Literary Texts*, Toronto, 1975 |
| *BiOr* | *Bibliotheca Orientalis* |
| *BSOAS* | *Bulletin of the School of Oriental and African Studies* |
| *CDAFI* | *Cahiers de la Délégation Française en Iran* |
| *GM* | *Göttinger Miszellen* |
| *IstMitt* | *Istanbuler Mitteilungen* |
| *JCS* | *Journal of Cuneiform Studies* |
| *JHS* | *Journal of Hellenic Studies* |
| *NABU* | *Notes assyriologiques brèves et utilitaires* |
| *NC* | *Numismatic Chronicle* |
| NS | New Series |
| *ÖAW* | *Österreichische Akademie der Wissenschaften* |
| *RA* | *Revue d'Assyriologie* |
| *TCL* | *Textes cunéiformes du Louvre*, Paris |
| *VDI* | *Vestnik Drevnei Istorii* |
| *YOS* | *Yale Oriental Series, Babylonian Texts*, New Haven, Conn. |

# 'GREEKS' AND 'GREECE' IN MESOPOTAMIAN AND PERSIAN PERSPECTVES[*]

MR. WARDEN, FELLOWS, LADIES AND GENTLEMEN,

Having accepted the invitation to give the Sir John Myres Memorial Lecture, I was faced with the problem of what topic to choose for my talk, that might be deemed appropriate given his particular interests. As I cast about in my mind (somewhat desperately), I recalled — from the very first term of my very first year as an undergraduate — a vignette Myres draws at the beginning of his book on Herodotus: he pictured the future historian in 480 as a five-year old, watching with his mother the Carian arm of the Persian forces limping home from Greece in tatters and asking 'What is it all about?'[1] Myres' picture is that of a Greek, on the cusp of two worlds, puzzling about the clash between two separate spheres — east and west. This prompted me to think a bit more about the question of perceptions, particularly the problems inherent in trying to define what 'the east' may have thought about 'the west', and Greeks, in particular, at different periods.

In recent years — and this is linked to the much larger debates about what it means to be British, English or European[2] and the wider questions of western intellectual and cultural imperialism in the wake of decolonisation[3] — studies of Greek perceptions of 'non-Greeks' have become something of a growth industry among classical historians, basing themselves on the rich and diverse surviving literary heritage.[4] And it has been most fruitfully fuelled by anthropological and sociological approaches to ethnicity, to self-definition through the mirror of 'otherness', to stereotyping, and by the application of models such as

---

[*] I should like to thank Professor Robert Parker and the Sir John Myres Committee in Oxford for inviting me to deliver this memorial lecture, and the family of Sir John Myres for endowing it. I must also thank Emma Dench (Birkbeck College, London) for helpful discussion on topics relating to the subject of my talk.

1 J. L. Myres, *Herodotus, Father of History*, Oxford, 1953.

2 See, for example, L. Colley, *Britons: forging the nation 1707–1837*, New Haven, Conn., 1992. Also note the recent article by S. Sandhu, 'Bringing the empire home', *Times Literary Supplement*, 16 March, 2001, 8.

3 Best known, of course, are E. Said, *Orientalism*, London, 1978, and *Culture and Imperialism*, London, 1993, as well as M. Bernal, *Black Athena: the Afro-Asiatic roots of classical civilization I: the fabrication of ancient Greece 1785–1985*, London, 1987.

4 A random selection of some recent publications includes: E. Hall, *Inventing the Barbarian: Greek self-definition through tragedy*, Oxford, 1989. Idem, 'Asia unmanned: images of victory in classical Athens', in J. Rich and G. Shipley, eds., *War and Society in the Greek World*, London, 1993, 107–33. P. Cartledge, *The Greeks: a portrait of self and others*, Oxford, 1993. J. E. Coleman and C. A. Waltz, eds., *Greeks and Barbarians: essays on the interactions between Greeks and non-Greeks in antiquity and the consequences for Eurocentrism,* (Occasional Publications of the Department of Near Eastern Studies and the Program of Jewish Studies, Cornell University 4), Bethesda, MD, 1997. T. Harrison, *The Emptiness of Asia: Aeschylus'* Persians *and the history of the fifth century*, London, 2000. Note also the collection of readings on the subject edited by T. Harrison, *Greeks and Barbarians*, Edinburgh, 2001.

Benedict Anderson's 'imagined communities'.[5] These have helped to highlight the way identities are not static 'givens', but unstable, subject to a continuous process of negotiation — in short contested arenas that are historically grounded.[6] Within these discussions, some of the eastern neighbours of Greece, particularly the Persians, have provided the generally negative norms against which processes of Greek self-definition were played out.[7] And these processes are complex, operating as they do on multiple levels. As Margaret Miller has shown in her recent book, for example, Athenians in the fifth century had a profound familiarity with things Persian, adopting and adapting many items of Persia's distinctive, élite cultural inventory for use in the context of Athenian civic and social life, to mark internal divisions of status. Yet at the public level of political self-representation, where Athens cast itself in the role of leader of the 'free world' against Persian 'oppression' the Athenian stance was, of course, one of total rejection of anything Persian, a complete contrast was drawn between the effeminate, slavish Persian subject ruled by a despot and the manly, free Athenian.[8] Simultaneously, as Michael Whitby has persuasively argued, Greek élites, within and beyond the north-western frontiers of the Persian empire, maintained very active relations with each other, sedulously cultivating their connections with the royal and satrapal courts.[9] So the interplay of Greeks and Persians is an intricate one, and by no means unidirectional. But if we turn to the question of how some of Greece's eastern neighbours might have regarded Greeks, how they were accommodated into their global visions and what roles they played within them, we are faced with the problem that, while we can hear the Greek side of such dialogues fairly clearly, the eastern one is elusive to the point of apparent muteness. Yet I think that, despite the difficulties, it may be possible to gain some insights.

The task is certainly not an easy one and will, of necessity, have to be restricted in chronological and geographical scope. The period I shall concentrate on is that of the eighth to third centuries B.C., when the then 'known world' (Figure 5) was, more or less, dominated, successively, by the Neo-Assyrian, Neo-Babylonian, Achaemenid Persian and hellenistic Macedonian empires. The evidence I shall use comes mainly from Mesopotamia and from Persian royal

5 B. Anderson, *Imagined Communities: reflections on the origin and spread of nationalism,* (rev. ed), London, 1991.

6 See, for example, J. Hall, *Ethnic Identity in Greek Antiquity*, Cambridge, 1997, and note the review by E. Dench (*Classical Review*, 50/1, 2000, 210–11) with its helpful remarks on the problems raised by 'excessive obedience' to modern anthropological theories.

7 Note, in this context, P. Briant, 'Histoire et idéologie: les Grecs et la "decadence perse"', in M. -M. Mactoux and E. Geny, édd., *Mélanges P. Lévêque*, Besançon, 1989, II, 33–47 (now translated in the volume edited by Harrison, 2001, above n. 4).

8 M. C. Miller, *Persia and Athens in the Fifth Century: a study in cultural receptivity*, Cambridge, 1997.

9 M. Whitby, 'An international symposium? Ion of Chios fr.27 and the margins of the Delian League', in E. Dabrowa, ed., *Ancient Iran and the Mediterranean World*, Uniwersytet Jagiellonski: Studies in Ancient History, 2, Kraków, 207–24.

centres. The greatest problem is presented by the lack of discursive writings and descriptive narratives of the type produced in the Greek and later Roman worlds, genres familiar to us. Instead the main corpus of evidence is made up of allusions in formal, public royal proclamations, brief references in chronicles, king-lists, diaries and scholarly texts and the appearance of Greeks in various administrative and business documents. Although not extensive, this material can, I think, reveal a range of perspectives and voices as the political and socio-economic relationships of Greek communities with the world of these large eastern states shifted and intensified, bringing profound transformations in their wake.[10] An important aspect, which it is crucially important to define, is the mental maps into which Assyrians, Babylonians and Persians slotted the Greeks they came into contact with: what space do they occupy in these symbolic universes? What role are they allotted in such imagined worlds? In order to try to pin-point these issues, I shall begin by outlining the political changes, the evidence for Greek interactions with the Mesopotamian, Persian and Seleucid realms and then, against that background, look at what images emerge, why and when they change.

## The political scene (Figure 4)

In the second half of the eighth century B.C., the concept of an 'Ionian' land appears in some Assyrian texts. Its inhabitants are most usually called 'Ionians', or people from 'Ionia'. To what extent this may already define 'Greeks' in a specific linguistic or cultural sense is unclear; certainly it reflects the fact that there were encounters with, and knowledge of, residents of a region in Western Turkey.[11] Ionian comes to be the normal terminology for Greeks, widely used, and when we encounter a deviation from this, I shall suggest that that is significant. Throughout, of course, we need to be aware of the hard realities: i.e. that the Aegean and Near Eastern spheres are not distinct, contrasting entities: the enormously diverse eastern world needs to be visualized as a mosaic of highly

10 For introductions to the Neo-Assyrian, Neo-Babylonian and Achaemenid empires, see A. Kuhrt, *The Ancient Near East, c.3000–330 B.C.*, London, 1995, chs. 9, 11 and 13. For a detailed study of the Neo-Assyrian empire, see F. M. Fales, *L'impero assiro*, Rome, 2001. For the Neo-Babylonian empire, F. Joannès, *La Mésopotamie au 1er millénaire avant J. -C.*, Paris, 2000, chs. 5 and 6, provides a brief but excellent discussion. The fundamental study of Achaemenid history and institutions is P. Briant, *Histoire de l'empire perse: de Cyrus à Alexandre*, Paris, 1996. The most recent general study of hellenistic history is G. Shipley, *The Greek World after Alexander, 323–30 B.C.*, London, 2000. For the Seleucid empire, see E. Bickerman, *Institutions séleucides*, Paris, 1938. A. Kuhrt and S. Sherwin-White, eds., *Hellenism in the East: the interaction of Greek and non-Greek civilizations from Syria to Central Asia after Alexander*, London, 1987. S. Sherwin-White and A. Kuhrt, *From Samarkhand to Sardis: a new approach to the Seleucid empire*, London, 1993.

11 The evidence is surveyed and the philological problems explored by J. A. Brinkman, 'The Akkadian words for "Ionia" and "Ionian"', in *Daidalikon: Studies in honor of Raymond V. Schoder, S.J.*, Waucoda, Ill. 1989, 53–71. Some of his reservations are challenged (persuasively) and more examples adduced by R. Rollinger, 'Zur Bezeichnung von "Griechen" in Keilschrifttexten', *RA*, 91, 1997 [1999], 167–72.

individual and distinctive cultures, which had overlapped and interacted more and less intensely over several thousand years by the time of the eighth century. Moreover, as far as the evidence can be traced back, the Aegean communities had always been vitally involved in this political, economic and cultural interplay, as has been richly demonstrated, most recently in the works of Stephanie Dalley and Martin West.[12]

To set the various eastern definitions of Greeks into perspective, let me just outline briefly the political developments of the period I am concerned with. From 745 on, the Assyrian empire expanded to control, either directly or indirectly, the territory from the shores of the Persian Gulf to Central Anatolia, the Zagros mountains to the Egyptian frontier and the terminal points of the Arabian caravan routes. Its immediate neighbours in the north and north-west were Urartu (Armenia) and Phrygia, the latter replaced by the burgeoning power of Lydia in the 670s. When the Babylonians, with help from the Median federation to the east, defeated the Assyrians in the 620s and 610s, they inherited virtually all of Assyria's imperial territories. Despite a shift south of the political centre, the establishment of a Babylonian dynasty and a different political rhetoric, the fairly short-lived Neo-Babylonian empire (626–539) represents, in essence, a continuum with the preceding Assyrian one. Following the lightning campaigns of expansion mounted by the Persian kings, Cyrus and Cambyses, between 550 and 522, the geo-political picture changed fundamentally: by 520, no political entity with the potential to challenge Persian power effectively survived; Darius I and Xerxes successfully consolidated these conquests. The Achaemenid dynasty commanded an empire of unrivalled size for over 200 years, until Alexander of Macedon mounted his extraordinary invasion, which began in 334 and ended in his death in Babylon in 323. While the reasons for his success are still debated, what is clear is that the integrity of the empire crumbled quickly with Alexander's death.[13] By 280, it had been replaced by three major powers, centred on the Fertile Crescent (Seleucids), Egypt (Ptolemies) and Macedon itself (Antigonids) — all three locked in constant, deadly competition, while many regions, east and west, developed into smaller independent kingdoms and polities, in uneasy and shifting alliance with the larger states.

---

12 S. Dalley, ed., *The Legacy of Mesopotamia*, Oxford, 1998. M. L. West, *The East Face of Helicon: West Asiatic elements in Greek poetry and myth*, Oxford, 1997. Note also some earlier studies, such as W. Burkert, *The Orientalizing Revolution: Near Eastern influence on Greek culture in the early Archaic Age*, (trans.), Cambridge, Mass. 1992. S. P. Morris, *Daidalos and the Origins of Greek Art*, Princeton, N.J., 1992. C. Penglase, *Greek Myths and Mesopotamia: parallels and influence in the Homeric Hymns and Hesiod*, London, 1994. See also R. Osborne, *Greece in the Making, 1200–479 B.C.*, London, 1996, 104–29 (discussion of the early Greek alphabets on pp.107–12).

13 Pierre Briant has formulated the, to my mind, most fruitful approach to this historical phase. See his *Alexandre le Grand*, (Que sais-je? 4e éd.), Paris, 1994, and his *Histoire* (above n. 10), ch. 13 and pp.893–6. He is currently preparing a monograph on Darius III.

## The realities of Greek relations with the east

It is against this backdrop of fundamental, sometimes devastating and brutal, political changes, that I shall try to examine perceptions of Greeks in the Mesopotamian and Persian milieu. As is so often the case, definitions and images change depending on context: i.e., who is speaking to whom, when and for what purpose. First, let me outline some of the realities of Greek relations with these empires. Lanfranchi has recently argued,[14] on the basis of archaeological evidence combined with some epigraphic references, that in the late eighth and early seventh centuries, Assyrian kings encountered some (probably) East Greek groups serving as military allies of the Phrygian kingdom, whose ruler was challenging, unsuccessfully, Assyrian domination over Cilicia. Following Assyria's repulse of Phrygia's attempts to advance its borders, he argues, Phoenician merchants, who had been dominant in the Cilician area until this point, began to lose out to Greek trading networks in the Eastern Mediterranean, a fact reflected by the establishment of Greek settlements in North Syria and Cilicia in the wake of tightened Assyrian control.[15] All this coincides with the appearance of North Syrian, Phrygian and Urartian material on some East Greek sites. The cumulative evidence would thus suggest, in his view, that some Greeks lived as Assyrian subjects inside the empire itself;[16] their labour may even have been harnessed by the Assyrian king, Sennacherib, in the preparation of a campaign to the Persian Gulf,[17] although this idea depends on a single, contested reading.[18] What is more certain is that, simultaneously, the élites of several major Levantine cities, both on the coast and inland, were importing, in increasing quantitites, certain types of Greek ceramics.[19] The shapes are limited and seem to reflect quite specific demands for, and a conscious selection by, segments of the local population of particular Greek pottery types for use within their own style of banqueting.[20] This, in turn, suggests the existence of some quite close contacts between Greek and Syro-Palestinian communities.

14 G. B. Lanfranchi, 'The ideological and political impact of the Assyrian cultural imperial expansion on the Greek world in the 8th and 7th centuries B.C.', in S. Aro and R. M. Whiting, eds., *The Heirs of Assyria* (Melammu Symposia 1), Helsinki, 7– 34.

15 Recent discussions of the vexed question of the nature and date of Greek settlement here (with full references) are: J. Boardman, 'The excavated history of Al Mina', in G. Tsetskhladze, ed., *Ancient Greeks West and East,* (Mnemosyne Suppl. 196), Leiden, 1999, 135–62. R. A. Kearsley, 'Greeks overseas in the eighth century B.C.: Euboeans, Al Mina and Assyrian imperialism', *ibid.*, 109–34. T. Hodos, 'Kinet Höyük and Al Mina: new views on old relationships', in *Periplous: papers on classical art and archaeology presented to Sir John Boardman*, London, 2000, 145–52.

16 *Cf.* also, somewhat less confidently, R. Rollinger, 1997 (above n. 11).

17 G. B. Lanfranchi, 2000 (above n. 14), 28–9.

18 See E. Frahm, *Einleitung in die Sanherib-Inschriften,* (AfO Beih. 26), Vienna, 1997, 117b Z.60.

19 J. Waldbaum, 'Early Greek contacts with the Southern Levant, *c.*1000–600 B.C.: the eastern perspective', *BASOR,* 293 (1994), 53–66.

20 J. Waldbaum, 'Greeks *in* the East or Greeks *and* the East? Problems in the definition and recognition of presence', *BASOR,* 305 (1997), 1–17.

Somewhere into this, of course, also needs to be set the Greek adoption of the Phoenician alphabet, and the strong echoes of eastern literary motifs in Greek compositions.[21] The interpretation of much of the evidence, and how to weight it precisely, is highly contentious; nevertheless, interactions of a rather complex, even intimate, kind are undeniable.

The situation is somewhat clearer at the time of the Neo-Babylonian empire. A collection of texts from Nebuchadnezzar's reign, listing rations distributed to personnel in the palace at Babylon, shows that his cosmopolitan court included workers, probably carpenters, from Ionia, although their names are not recognisable as Greek.[22] But the reality of Greeks in Babylonian service is beautifully caught in Alkaios' poem welcoming his brother, Antimenidas, back from service in Nebuchadnezzar's army and bringing with him the gold-bound sword, with which he had been rewarded for an act of outstanding bravery.[23] Business documents from the same period show that substantial quantities of bronze and iron were being imported from the Aegean into Babylonia. One text also refers to the issue of Ionian purple wool to Babylonian weavers, although this may simply be a way of describing a particular type of wool, rather than indicating Ionia/Greece as its direct source — somewhat as we talk about 'tweed' or 'angora wool'.[24]

With the Persian empire, the nature of Greek relations with the larger world to the east intensified: many Greek cities were subject to Persian satraps; innumerable European Greeks travelled on embassies to the royal, as well as provincial, courts to solicit financial and political aid or seek asylum; Persia provided a ready source of gainful employment for Greek soldiers, craftsmen, doctors; the populations of some Greek centres were deported and resettled as coherent communities — the places attested are Central Asia and Babylonia — while Greek prisoners of war swelled the labour force of royal capitals in Fars, were sold as slaves or became the concubines of Persian nobles.[25] Although the evidence is not immense, there are also indications of intermarriage between the

21  For an exhaustive exploration of these, see M. L. West, 1997 (above n. 12).

22  E. F. Weidner, 'Jojachin, König von Juda, in babylonischen Keilschrifttexten', *Mélanges syriens offerts à Monsieur René Dussaud*, Paris, 1939, II, 923–35.

23  *Greek Lyric*, I (Loeb Classical Library), Cambridge, Mass., 1982, Alkaios no. 350.

24  *TCL*, 12, 84 (dated 14.11.551) and *YOS*, 6, 168 (dated 15.10.550) concern imports of bronze and iron. *YOS*, 17, 253 (dated 29.4.601) mentions 'purple wool of Ionia' issued to weavers in Uruk. The documents are translated and commented by A. L. Oppenheim, 'An essay on overland trade in the first millennium B.C.', *JCS,* 21 (1967), 236–54. One other reference occurs in a fragmentary chronicle (BM 33041), which deals with Nebuchadnezzar II's invasion of Egypt in 568. A place called 'Putu-Yaman' appears here, which E. Edel ('Amasis und Nebukadrezar II', *GM,* 29 (1978), 13–20) has argued refers to Cyrene, here called 'Libya of the Ionians'.

25  For a prosopography, see J. Hofstetter, *Die Griechen in Persien: Prosopographie der Griechen im Persischen Reich vor Alexander,* (*AMI* Ergänzungsband 5), Berlin, 1978. Note also the remarks by D. M. Lewis, *Sparta and Persia,* (Cincinnati Classical Studies, N.S. 1), Leiden, 1977, 12–15, and the article by J. Nollé and A. Wenninger, 'Themistokles und Archepolis: eine griechische Dynastie im Perserreich und ihre Münzprägung', *Jahrbuch für Numismatik und Geldgeschichte,* 48/49, 1998/1999 [2001], 29–70.

élites of Greek cities and Persians.[26] The material evidence, too, echoes some of these varied and intense interactions: Greek motifs appear on traditional Babylonian seals, impressed on tablets written in Babylonian cuneiform and used by Babylonians in their internal affairs; work in Greek style is commissioned by local dynasts in the Levant; Greek pottery continues to be imported; Greek coins are found on several sites in the empire, including Persepolis; certain Greek techniques are exploited for the construction of Persian palaces.[27]

These trends continue in the Seleucid period, although there are changes, too, as Greek-Macedonians form the dominant, ruling élite; some individuals in Babylonian cities adopt Greek names in addition to their indigenous ones; some local scholars compose historical accounts of their region in Greek, for their new rulers, employing Greek ideas of historiography; many Greek cities send out settlers to swell the population of new urban centres in Mesopotamia, Persis and Central Asia; the number of Graeco-Macedonian soldiers settled in military colonies increases.[28] There is also at this time some slight, but interesting Babylonian evidence suggesting a reactive emphasis on local traditions.[29] The impression, here, is of a long-term dialogue, in the course of which Babylonian identities are redefined. What emerges from this brief survey, and this needs to be stressed, is the long familiarity of the rulers and inhabitants of the Mesopotamian and Persian empires with many details of Greek culture and vice-versa.

## Imagery and Mental Maps

These are the realities: but realities are one thing, political rhetoric and the representations of power are quite other, operating at a different level where mental imagery determines the picture of one's own place in the world and that

26 See most recently M. Whitby, 1998 (above n. 9).

27 In general on this topic, see M. C. Root, 'From the heart: powerful Persianisms in the art of the of the Western Empire', *AchHist,* VI (1991), 1–29. M. C. Miller 1997 (above n. 8). J. Boardman, *Persia and the West: an archaeological investigation on the genesis of Achaemenid Persian art,* London, 2000. For use of Greek style seals on Persian period Babylonian tablets, see L. Jakob-Rost and H. Freydank, 'Spätbabylonische Rechtsurkunden aus Babylon mit aramäischen Beischriften', *Forschungen und Berichte der Staatlichen Museen zu Berlin,* 14 (1972), 7–35. See also D. Collon, 'A hoard of sealings from Ur', in M. -F. Boussac and A. Invernizzi, eds., *Archives et sceaux du monde hellénistique,* (B.C.H, Supp. 29), Athens, Paris, 1997, 65–84 and the review by A. Kuhrt of R. Wallenfels, *Uruk: Hellenistic Seal Impressions in the Yale Babylonian Collection. I: Cuneiform Tablets,* (Ausgrabungen in Uruk-Warka, 19), Mainz, 1994 in *BiOr,* 56 (1999), 449–54, citing further examples. For masons from western Asia Minor in Persis, see C. Nylander, *Ionians in Pasargadae: studies in Old Persian architecture*, Uppsala, 1970. For Greek coins in the Persepolis deposit, see discussion by M. C. Root, 'Evidence from Persepolis for the dating of Persian and Archaic Greek coinage', *NC,* 1988, 1–12. For the Sidon sarcophagi, see V. von Graeve, *Der Alexandersarkophag und seine Werkstatt,* Berlin, 1970. *Cf.* J. Frel, 'The Rhodian workmanship of the Alexander sarcophagus', *IstMitt,* 21 (1971), 121–24.

28 See the discussions in A. Kuhrt and S. Sherwin-White 1987 and 1993, esp. ch. 6 (above n. 10), and T. Boiy, *Laatachemenidisch en hellenistisch Babylon: portret van een mesopatische stad in een cultureel spanningsveld,* (PhD Leuven, 2000), 264–67. Also P. Briant, 'Colonizzazione ellenistica e popolazioni del Vicino Oriente: dinamiche sociali e politiche di acculturazione', in S. Settis, ed., *I Greci: Storia-Cultura-Arte-Società, 2: una storia greca III. Trasformazioni,* Rome, 1998, 309–33.

29 See the study by R. Wallenfels and the review cited above, n. 27.

of others.[30] We, therefore, need to try to define the geographical visions current in Mesopotamia and Persia during this span of nearly five hundred years.

## a – Assyria and Babylonia

Ideas about the shape and structure of the world, the locating of places within it, had a long tradition in the shared cultures of Babylonia and Assyria, although the southern, Babylonian viewpoint seems always to have been the dominant one. It was linked to mythical, legendary and heroic figures: gods had created the world, epic heroes and great kings of the past had traversed its difficult terrain, encircled and conquered it. The universe consisted of three levels of the heavens — sky, the middle heavens and the highest heaven; beneath the sky was the surface of the earth, below that, the *apsu*, source of fertile, sweet waters and the home of Ea, a crafty deity and friend of man; below this again was the underworld, realm of the dead (Figure 1a). The earth's surface was pictured in a variety of ways, yet certain basic elements seem to remain fairly constant and are attested in two texts current in this period.

One (Figure 1b) describes the 'totality of the land under heaven', which the great warrior-king, Sargon of Akkad, who reigned *c*.2300 B.C. and became the example *par excellence* of the world-conqueror, is said to have ruled over.[31] It presents a late scholarly reconstruction of his empire, centred on the city of Akkad, with distances between different places measured and its frontiers fixed: the Assyrian-Babylonian realm lies at the core; to the east are the regions of Iran; to the north-west is the Cedar Mountain, with the land of Hana beyond; to the south-west are the Arabian desert and Egypt; beyond the Mediterranean (Upper Sea) lie the tin country and Crete; in the Persian Gulf (Lower Sea) are Dilmun (Bahrain) and Magan (Oman). Towards the end of the text, various people are briefly described, who diverge from the norms of civilized behaviour, in terms of dress, treatment of the dead and cuisine. Some place names hover on the edge between the known and unknown, and may, in essence, be utopian, e.g. Baza;[32] but where they are not, quite a few are archaic and no longer in contemporary

---

30 See the acute remarks by P. Michalowski, 'Mental maps and ideology: reflections on Subartu', in H. Weiss ed., *The Origins of Cities in Dry-Farming Syria and Mesopotamia in the Third Millennium B.C.*, Gilford, 1986, 129–56, and by G. Jonker, *The Topography of Remembrance: the dead, tradition and collective memory in Mesopotamia,* (Studies in the History of Religions, 68), Leiden, 1995, esp. 35–47.

31 Transliteration, translation and detailed commentary in W. Horowitz, *Mesopotamian Cosmic Geography* (Mesopotamian Civilizations, 8), Winona Lake, IN, 1998, 67–95. *Cf.* also the comments by G. Jonker, 1995 (above n. 29), 41–4. For the crucial political-ideological role of Sargon in Mesopotamian history and historiography, see the essays by M. Liverani and P. Michalowski in M. Liverani, ed., *Akkad the First World Empire: structure, ideology, traditions,* (History of the Ancient Near East, Studies V), Padua, 1993, 41–67, 69–90. J. G. Westenholz, 'Heroes of Akkad', *JAOS*, 103 (1983), 327–36. G. Jonker, 1995 (above n. 30) *passim.*

32 Baza/u's precise location remains uncertain, although somewhere in North Arabia is implied. Apart from here, it only appears in texts of Esarhaddon (R. Borger, *Die Inschriften Asarhaddons, Königs von Assyrien,* (AfO Beih., 9), Graz, 1956, 33:26, 56:53, 57:76, 86 no.57:4) as a vast hostile terrain, traversed and measured by the heroic Assyrian king in the course of an epic sortie into new and exotic territory. *Cf.* F. M. Fales, 2001 (above n. 10), 26–7.

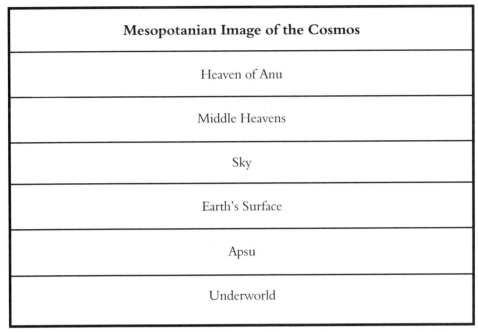

| Mesopotanian Image of the Cosmos |
|---|
| Heaven of Anu |
| Middle Heavens |
| Sky |
| Earth's Surface |
| Apsu |
| Underworld |

Figure 1a — Mesopotamian Image of the Cosmos (after W. Horowitz, 1998)

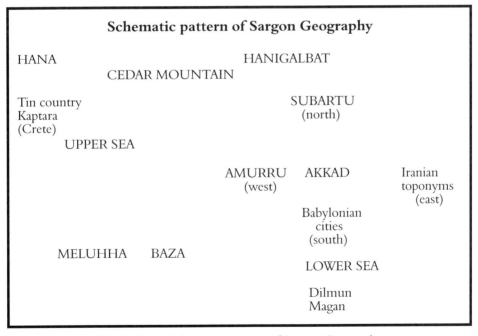

**Schematic pattern of Sargon Geography**

HANA                    HANIGALBAT
         CEDAR MOUNTAIN

Tin country               SUBARTU
Kaptara                 (north)
(Crete)
    UPPER SEA

             AMURRU   AKKAD     Iranian
             (west)         toponyms
                       (east)

                Babylonian
                cities
                (south)

MELUHHA   BAZA          LOWER SEA

                Dilmun
                Magan

Figure 1b — Schematic pattern of Sargon Geography

use; they have been shifted away from their original locations to designate quite different, distant regions: e.g., Hanigalbat, which had been the name of a country in Upper Mesopotamia in the second millennium, is used to describe the area approximately of Armenia;[33] and Meluhha in the late third millennium designated the Indus valley, but here it is applied to the Nubian-Egyptian realm. Hana, in the first half of the second millennium, was the name of a tribal group, associated later with a small kingdom, located on the Middle Euphrates;[34] yet in this text, it designates a far distant region beyond the wondrous 'Cedar Mountain', which lies somewhere away in the highlands of Central Turkey. The shape of this world seems to be a rough rectangle or trapezoid, with a known, and knowable, civilized centre bordered by distant barbarian regions. The use of antique toponyms to signal them serves to indicate that in these foreign, wondrous parts, beyond the ken of the present day, time has stood still.[35]

A somewhat different image, although analogous in its fundamental vision, is the 'Babylonian *mappa mundi*' (Figure 2), presenting a captioned diagram and accompanying commentary.[36] The inner circle depicts the reasonably known and familiar world, with Babylon on the Euphrates picked out as the chief centre. The bitter sea surrounds this portion of earth and beyond it were, originally, perhaps seven narrow triangular 'distant regions' (*nagû*). These are described in the commentary as places, difficult of access, inhabited by strange creatures, dangerous, some of them cloaked in darkness; there is a hint that travellers might run the risk of falling into the underworld trying to reach them. Only a couple of legendary figures of the distant past and, again, the great Sargon of Akkad are associated with these far-off realms.[37]

33 Note, for example, that a Babylonian astronomical diary (A. J. Sachs and H. Hunger, *Astronomical Diaries and Related Texts from Babylonia*, (3 vols, ÖAW, Phil.-hist. Kl., Denkschr.), Vienna, 1988–96, II, no. –164, B 15) describes Antiochus IV campaigning, in 165/4, in the Land of Hanigalbat, which, in this instance, means Armenia.

34 The crucial discussions of the geographical name and its meaning in the second millennium are: W. Röllig, 'Aspects of the historical geography of northeastern Syria from Middle Assyrian to Neo-Assyrian times', in S. Parpola and R. M. Whiting, eds., *Assyria 1995*, Helsinki, 1997, 281–93 (289–90). D. Charpin, 'À propos des rois de Hana', *NABU*, 1995, no. 23. M. Luciani, 'Again on DeZ 3281, Middle Assyrian toponymy and a *līmu* from Tell Šēh Hamad/*Dūr Katlimmu*', *NABU*, 2001, no. 2. For the history of the 'Kingdom of Hana', see A. Podany, 'A Middle Babylonian date for the Hana Kingdom', *JCS*, 43–5 (1991–3), 39–51. *Idem*, 'Some shared traditions between Hana and the Kassites', in *Crossing Boundaries and Linking Horizons: Studies in Honor of Michael Astour*, Bethesda, MD, 1998, 417–32.

35 P. Machinist, 'On self-consciousness in Mesopotamia', in S. N. Eisenstadt, ed., *The Origins and Diversity of Axial Age Civilizations*, New York, 1986, 183–202.

36 Transliteration, translation and commentary in W. Horowitz, 1998 (above n. 31), 20–42 (an earlier version was published as 'The Babylonian map of the world', *Iraq*, 50 (1988), 147–66). *Cf.* the discussion by G. Jonker, 1995 (above n. 30), 44–7.

37 W. Horowitz, 1998 (above n. 31), 22–3, l.10. The other two heroes of the past are, first, Uta-napishti, the Babylonian flood hero, who was granted eternal life and settled 'where the rivers flow forth' (i.e. the ends of the earth), see A. George, *The Epic of Gilgamesh: a new translation*, London, 1999, 95, XI 202–05. The second is Nur-Dagan of Purušhanda (in Anatolia), who figures as the opponent of Sargon of Akkad in the epic 'King of Battle'. The poem describes the immensely long and hazardous journey Sargon will have to make to reach Nur-Dagan's fabulously rich kingdom, see J. G. Westenholz, *Legends of the Kings of Akkade: the texts*, Winona Lake, IN, 1997, 118–21, ll. 24–35.

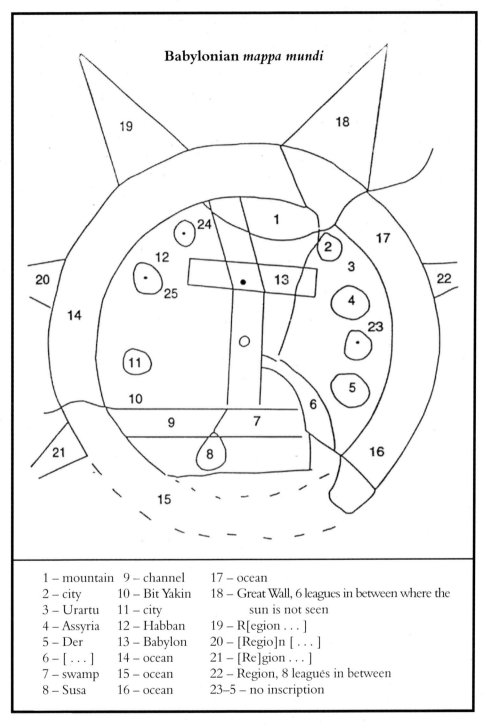

**Babylonian *mappa mundi***

| | | |
|---|---|---|
| 1 – mountain | 9 – channel | 17 – ocean |
| 2 – city | 10 – Bit Yakin | 18 – Great Wall, 6 leagues in between where the |
| 3 – Urartu | 11 – city | sun is not seen |
| 4 – Assyria | 12 – Habban | 19 – R[egion . . . ] |
| 5 – Der | 13 – Babylon | 20 – [Regio]n [ . . . ] |
| 6 – [ . . . ] | 14 – ocean | 21 – [Re]gion . . . ] |
| 7 – swamp | 15 – ocean | 22 – Region, 8 leagues in between |
| 8 – Susa | 16 – ocean | 23–5 – no inscription |

Figure 2 — Babylonian *mappa mundi* (after W. Horowitz, 1998)

These are the kinds of mental pictures that underlie and help to pattern the language and visual imagery of conquest and dominion deployed by Neo-Assyrian and Neo-Babylonian kings.[38] The Assyrian monarchs in particular employ it to vivid effect, penetrating ever further into distant lands, previously unknown and sometimes located 'beyond' or 'in the midst of the sea', images echoed in the language of the inscriptions of the later Babylonian kings, Nebuchadnezzar II and Nabonidus.[39] Thus some time around 730, King Tiglathpileser III, the first to extend Assyria's direct control signficantly, is described as follows:

> 'From the Bitter Sea of Yakin (marshes of S. Iraq) to Mount Bikni (Iran) in the east up to the Upper Sea of the west to Egypt, from the horizons to the heights of heaven, he ruled over countries.'[40]

Here the world girdled by the 'bitter sea' of the *mappa mundi* is embraced by the all-conquering Assyrian hero, who is now permanent master of the whole earth.[41] His successors push this territorial mastery further into some of the scarcely known, dangerous regions just beyond: they claim allegiance from islands in the Persian Gulf, from Phrygia to the north-west; they penetrate the Arabian desert, a legendary landscape filled with strange stones and poisonous reptiles and cross the hostile Sinai region to conquer Egypt and Nubia, imagined as frozen in time by attaching ancient toponyms to them: Magan and Meluhha.[42] When the last of the great Assyrian monarchs, Assurbanipal, evokes his power in the world, he describes Lydia, his north-western neighbour, with whom he shares a frontier and has a co-operative alliance, as 'a distant region (*nagû*) lying across the sea', in order to enhance the sense of Assyrian power sending forth its tentacles beyond the compass of the known and safe.[43] Added to the picture of an ever-widening Assyrian realm, is expansion into the Mediterranean to dominate 'the midst of the sea, from Cyprus, Ionia to Tarsos

---

38 Note particularly M. I. Marcus, 'Geography as visual ideology: landscape, knowledge, and power in Neo-Assyrian art', in M. Liverani, ed., *Neo-Assyrian Geography,* (Università di Roma 'La Sapienza', Dip. di Scienze storiche, archeologiche e antropologiche dell'Antichità, Quaderni di Geografia Storica 5), Rome, 1995, 193–202.

39 The references are collected in W. Horowitz, 1998 (above n. 31), 30–2. *Cf.* also B. Pongratz-Leisten, 'Toponyme als Ausdruck assyrischen Herrschaftsanspruch', in *Ana šadi Labnāni lū allik: Festschrift Wolfgang Röllig*, Neukirchen-Vluyn, 325–43.

40 H. Tadmor, *The Inscriptions of Tiglath-pileser III*, Jerusalem, 1994, 158, 3–4.

41 H. Tadmor, 'World dominion: the expanding horizon of the Assyrian empire', in L. Milano, S. de Martino, F. M. Fales and G. B. Lanfranchi, eds., *Landscapes: territories, frontiers and horizons in the ancient Near East (Papers presented to the XLIV Rencontre Assyriologique Internationale, Venezia, 7–11 July 1997)*, Part 1: *Invited Lectures,* (History of the Ancient Near East/Monographs III/1), Padua, 1999, 55–62 (56–7).

42 H. Tadmor, 1999 (above n. 41), 57–60.

43 M. Streck, *Assurbanipal*, Bd. 1–3 (Vorderasiatische Bibliothek, 7), Leipzig, 1916, 2: 20–1, 95–6. 166–7, 13–14.

(in Cilicia)'.[44] And it is here, in these dark, far away, mythical zones, that Sargon II says he 'caught Ionians of the midst of the sea like fish'.[45]

## b – The Persian empire

Although we have no comparable texts emanating from a scholarly milieu for the Achaemenid Persians, some important aspects of their vision of the world can be gleaned from their royal inscriptions. First, and most striking, is the strong emphasis placed on the ethnic identity of the king and the pre-eminent place occupied by Persia within the empire, which is equated with the world as a whole. Thus Darius I proclaims himself:

> 'I am Darius, the great king, king of kings, king of all kinds of peoples, king on this great earth far and wide, son of Hystaspes, an Achaemenid, a Persian, son of a Persian, an Aryan, having Aryan lineage.'[46]

Expressions of this kind appear for the first time with Darius in the context of his refoundation of Cyrus and Cambyses' empire, after a brief, but terrible, period of internal dissension, which threatened to tear it apart. After saving the realm from this crisis, the Persian king and Persia are presented, time and again, as the only source of rightful power, which has created order in, and for, the world. This places Persia 'a good country, possessed of good men, possessed of good horses',[47] at the centre of the imperial space. The countries ruled over have been seized by the Persian king, the 'Persian man' has gone forth and fought battles at the distant corners of the earth to create the prosperous tranquillity which now enfolds it.[48] And this image of Persia as the centre of the universe, part of the Iranian god, Ahuramazda's, bountiful creation, assigns its subjects their relative space in the cosmos. One of the recurring features of the royal inscriptions is a list of the countries and peoples over which the Achaemenid

44 R. Borger (above n. 32), 86, 10–11. Some, such as E. Lipiński, have argued that Tarsus here refers to Tartessus in Spain. See E. Lipiński, ed., *Dictionnaire de la Civilisation Phénicienne et Punique*, Turnhout, 1992, *s.v.* 'Tarshish'.

45 The references with discussion are usefully collected in J. A. Brinkman, 1989 (above n. 11), 55–6.

46 DNa 8-14. The basic edition of Old Persian royal inscriptions is R. G. Kent, *Old Persian: grammar, texts, lexicon,* (2nd ed.), New Haven, Conn. All inscriptions are normally cited in accordance with his system of sigla. Only one significantly new inscription has been added to the corpus since Kent's work, namely a quadrilingual one on the Darius statue found in Susa in 1973, given the siglum DSab (for full publication and discussion, see *CDAFI*, 4 (1974). New translations of all the inscriptions, including the Old Persian text on the Susa statue, are presented in P. Lecoq, *Les inscriptions de la Perse achéménide*, Paris, 1997. Complete new editions, translations and commentaries of the Old Persian inscriptions from Behistun, Persepolis and Naqsh-i Rustam are: R. Schmitt, *The Bisitun Inscriptions of Darius the Great*, (Corpus Inscriptionum Iranicarum, Part I, The Inscriptions of Ancient Iran, vol. I, The Old Persian Inscriptions. Texts I), London, 1991. *Idem, The Old Persian Inscriptions of Naqsh-i Rustam and Persepolis*, (Corpus Inscriptionum Iranicarum, Part I, The Inscriptions of Ancient Iran, vol. I, The Old Persian Inscriptions. Texts II), London, 2000.

47 DPd 7–9.

48 See DNa, paras 3–4. DSe para 4. Further discussion of the Achaemenid emphasis on the dominant position of Persians in the empire in P. Briant, 'De Samarkand à Sardes et de la ville de Suse au pays des Hanéens', *Topoi*, 4/1 (1994), 455–67 (460–1).

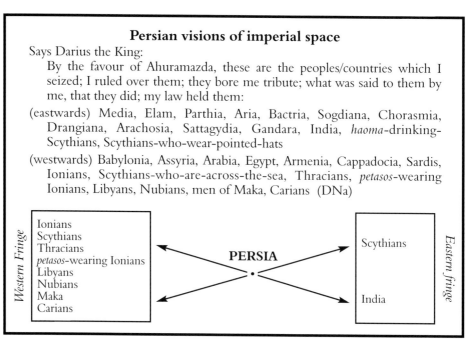

**Persian visions of imperial space**

Says Darius the King:

> By the favour of Ahuramazda, these are the peoples/countries which I seized; I ruled over them; they bore me tribute; what was said to them by me, that they did; my law held them:

(eastwards) Media, Elam, Parthia, Aria, Bactria, Sogdiana, Chorasmia, Drangiana, Arachosia, Sattagydia, Gandara, India, *haoma*-drinking-Scythians, Scythians-who-wear-pointed-hats

(westwards) Babylonia, Assyria, Arabia, Egypt, Armenia, Cappadocia, Sardis, Ionians, Scythians-who-are-across-the-sea, Thracians, *petasos*-wearing Ionians, Libyans, Nubians, men of Maka, Carians (DNa)

*Western Fringe*

Ionians
Scythians
Thracians
*petasos*-wearing Ionians
Libyans
Nubians
Maka
Carians

**PERSIA**

Scythians

India

*Eastern fringe*

Figure 3a — Persian visions of imperial space

king claims dominion (Figure 3a). The list always begins with those nearest the imperial centre in Persia, and then moves progressively outwards, enumerating all subjects up to the edges of the known world.[49] The order is not completely constant: the lists can start either with the eastern or the western part of the empire, but the movement is always out from the centre to the periphery.[50] This makes for a kind of ripple effect, with Persia as the perfect, still centre; and it is this image which may be reflected in Herodotus' statement (1.134) that the Persians:

> '. . . most of all hold themselves in honour, then those who dwell next to themselves, and then those next to them, and so on, so that there is a progression in honour in relation to the distance. They hold least in honour those whose habitation is furthest from their own. This is because they think themselves to be the best of mankind in everything and that others have a hold on virtue in proportion to their nearness; those who live furthest away are the most base.'

49 The one exception to this is Xerxes' 'daiva' inscription = XPh, para 3, *cf.* P. Lecoq, 1997 (above n. 46), 134. R. Schmitt, 2000 (above n. 46), 94, ad ll. 19–28.

50 The geographical order of the lists is discussed by M. C. Root, *The King and Kingship in Achaemenid Art: essays on the creation of an iconography of empire,* (Acta Iranica, 9), Leiden, 1979, 63–5. Their implications for the Achaemenid imperial vision is analysed by P. Briant, 1996 (above n. 10), 184–96.

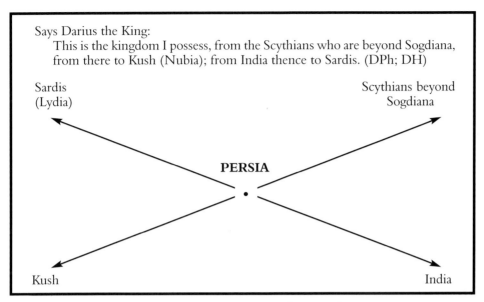

Says Darius the King:
   This is the kingdom I possess, from the Scythians who are beyond Sogdiana,
   from there to Kush (Nubia); from India thence to Sardis. (DPh; DH)

Sardis (Lydia)

Scythians beyond Sogdiana

**PERSIA**

Kush

India

Figure 3b — Persian visions of imperial space

If we now think about the place occupied by Greeks within such a mental scheme, it clear that it is on the distant outer margins. Yet, simultaneously, they are well known enough to be differentiated, because in listing his subjects the Persian king wants to drive home to his audience the multiplicity and variety of the peoples he has conquered, by underscoring how manifold is the creation now united under his rule. Ionians/Greeks inevitably appear, as you see (Figure 3a), soon after Lydia or Sardis, usually in the company of 'tribal' peoples such as Thracians and Scythians. Occasionally, they are described simply as 'Ionians', but more usually they are divided up into different groups: 'Ionians of the land', '(Ionians) who are on the sea and the peoples beyond the sea', '*petasos*-wearing Ionians,' so that the sense conveyed is of a people who are homogeneous in one respect, yet who are also geographically, topographically, sartorially and hence politically, fragmented, and thus have had to be individually 'seized' by the Persian king. One of these distinctions is also shown on the reliefs depicting subject peoples on the Achaemenid tomb reliefs: here Ionians are shown both with and without the *petasos* hat. But, interestingly, beyond the hat it is impossible to distinguish them from the Carians, indeed it would be quite impossible to do so were it not for the useful ethnic labels attached on some of the tomb reliefs. Their distinction from the Lydians, too, is slight.[51] If we think of a

51 E. F. Schmidt, *Persepolis III: the royal tombs and other monuments,* (Oriental Institute Publications, 70), Chicago, 1970, figs. 47, 49, lower and upper two registers respectively (the middle photographs are the clearest). Some of these points were made by the late Heleen Sancisi-Weerdenburg in 1997 at colloquia in Bandirme (Turkey) and Washington (USA). I am indebted to her for letting me have a copy of the draft text of her communication on these occasions. As far as I am aware, both colloquia are being published.

somewhat different visualization of the Achaemenid territorial span, one in which it is defined in broad strokes according to the points of the compass, intersecting at the Persian centre, we find the Ionians completely elided out (*cf.* Figure 3b):

> 'This is the kingdom I possess, from the Scythians, who are beyond Sogdiana, from there to Kush (i.e. Nubia), from India, thence to Sardis.'[52]

Here, as the Persian king contemplates his empire, gazing out from the centre to the four corners of the world, the Ionians, along with other north-western tribal groups, are not deemed distinctive enough to serve as a significant boundary marker.

## The Seleucids and Babylonia

This marginality of Greeks in the imagery of the eastern powers had to be revised and rethought in the wake of Alexander's conquest and the establishment of the successor kingdoms. In Babylonia, which became an important, strategic base, first for Alexander and subsequently one of the core regions of the Seleucid empire, we find some traces that echo the complexities of response to a situation where the Ionians, mentally located in distant, inaccessible regions, had now become the political masters and moved centre-stage. This process of redefinition was not simple or univocal, and it might be useful just to remind ourselves of what Babylonia went through in this period, to give us a sense of the political drama within which the accommodation with the new rulers had to be formulated.

The picture of Babylonia in the last decades of Persian rule is of a prosperous and thriving region, well integrated into the larger imperial structure, its main city, Babylon, housing a Persian style palace used on occasion by the king himself, its ancient temples and cults fully functional. It was the centre for Darius III's massive troop mobilization before the battle of Gaugamela in 331. After the Persian defeat there, and Darius' move into Iran, the Persian commander Mazaeus negotiated the surrender of Babylon to Alexander, who was then given a ceremonial welcome by the citizens. His acceptance of the surrender is marked, in both Graeco-Roman and Babylonian sources, by references to his appropriate worship of Bel-Marduk, chief god of city and country, and his orders to refurbish existing sanctuaries. Despite the political crisis created by Alexander's death in Babylon in 323, city and country appear to have been relatively tranquil under their Macedonian satraps for the first five to six years: Alexander's half-brother, Philip, seems to have been accepted as legitimate successor and work begun on the beautification of Babylonian cult-centres continued. According to the only slightly later account of Hieronymus of

---

52 DPh, para 2. DH, para 2.

Cardia (preserved in Diodorus Siculus, books 18 and 19, when Seleucus became satrap in 321/0, he worked hard to forge close links with the Babylonian population, establishing a network of personal relationships, perhaps through grants of land and tax immunities. But this relatively peaceful scene was disrupted in 317/6, when Antigonus, trying to recreate personally the integrity of the Achaemenid-Alexander empire, expelled Seleucus, who sought refuge in Egypt. Coinciding with this, King Philip and his wife Eurydice were assassinated and the nominal ruler of this immense, tottering structure was now the helpless infant Alexander IV. No Babylonian (nor any other) evidence indicates that Antigonus involved himself much with Babylonian affairs, beyond ensuring control. His ambitions lay, at that time, further west, where the rulers of Macedon, Thrace and Egypt posed the main threat to his plans. This, perhaps combined with the goodwill generated earlier, made it possible for Seleucus to make an attempt to claw back his satrapy in 312/1 with a tiny force. Certainly whatever Babylonian support he had was strengthened by Antigonus' violent response to Seleucus' invasions: Antigonus' forces sacked Babylonian towns and temples, and ravaged the countryside. The horrors suffered by the population during the, at least, three-year long struggle between Antigonid and Seleucid forces is vividly evoked by a Babylonian chronicle, which refers repeatedly to 'weeping and mourning' in response to the looting and burning. By contrast, Hieronymus describes Seleucus acting to shield the local population, taking protective measures and evacuating them for their security. And, by 305/4, Seleucus was firmly in control of Babylonia, and had also added the major part of the Iranian plateau to his dominion. In consequence, and in parallel with Alexander's other successors, he took the title of king, the infant Alexander and his mother having been murdered in 311. It was probably soon after this assumption of the royal title, that he founded Seleucia-Tigris, strategically located at the terminus of the overland-route linking the Mesopotamian plain with the Iranian plateau, to strengthen control of his newly-forged kingdom, which extended well into Central Asia by 302; North Syria was added after the defeat of Antigonus in 301, and late in the 280s, substantial parts of Asia Minor. By 281, Seleucus claimed dominion over territories from the Hellespont to Bactria. Although the evidence is fragmentary, enough survives to indicate that in the 290s Seleucus' crown prince, Antiochus, was active in Babylonia, restoring Babylonian cults after the devastations of war. When he succeeded his father, this effort of restoration was crowned by the completion of work on the main temples of Babylon (271) and Borsippa(268).[53]

---

53 For full discussion, with references, see S. Sherwin-White, 'Seleucid Babylonia: a case study for the installation and development of Greek rule', in A. Kuhrt and S. Sherwin-White, 1987 (above n. 10), 1–31. S. Sherwin-White and A. Kuhrt, 1993 (above n. 10), ch.1. A. Kuhrt and S. Sherwin-White, 'The transition from Achaemenid to Seleucid rule in Babylonia: revolution or evolution?', *AchHist,* VIII (1994), 311–27. T. Boiy, 2000 (above n. 27), 107–45. F. Joannès, 2000 (above n. 10), 143–63.

What vocabulary do the Babylonian texts deploy to mark these varied, sometimes bloody and brutal, encounters with their new rulers? The first thing to note are some continuities. The familiar term 'Ionian' is still used to designate things Greek in day-to-day contexts: thus, for example, we have a reference to a situation of economic crisis in Babylonia in 274/3, when payments had to be made using 'Ionian', i.e. Greek, copper coins (Figure 6a.1); an astronomical diary for 169/8 mentions celebrations mounted in Babylon on receiving the news of Antiochus IV's victory in Egypt: they are performed 'according to an Ionian, i.e. Greek, pattern' (Figure 6a.2).[54] Rather less clear is a reference in a chronicle (Figure 6a.3) to Seleucus I and Ionians in 282; the fragmentary passage may imply that it describes part of his army, although this is not certain. These are just some examples in which the Greek nature of certain practices and peoples are registered, and the terminology seems largely neutral.

Alongside this, we find references to Macedon and Macedonians, a completely new element in the geographical lexicon, which shows a very lively awareness of the precise identity of the new rulers. Thus, the so-called 'Diadochi Chronicle' (Figure 6b.1) describes someone, probably Antipater, crossing in 319/8 to Macedon and not returning; while in the subsequent year, King Philip is associated with affairs 'in Macedon'. There is a clear sense here that the locus of power has shifted to a new centre across the sea; the affairs of empire are now to be conducted from this distant shore. This emerges even more markedly in the entry of another chronicle (Figure 6b.2) recounting Seleucus' follow up to his victory over Lysimachus in 281, where he moves with his troops 'to Macedon, his land'. The expression is striking. At this point, Seleucus had been closely associated with Babylonia for forty years, in undisputed control of it for thirty, and acknowledged as its legitimate king for twenty-five. One of his chief, indeed earliest, royal city foundations was on Babylonian soil, and he had been instrumental in protecting the local population, and defending and supporting traditional Babylonian institutions. Yet, despite all Seleucus' overtures and patronage to which the local population seems to have responded with loyal, even enthusiastic, support, the writer reveals a clear consciousness that, however much Seleucus may be 'king of Babylon', in one sense his true place of origin, where he belongs, is a distant, foreign country.[55] This is mirrored by the introductory passage of Antiochus I's foundation cylinder from Borsippa (Figure 6b.3), which records in absolutely standard Akkadian, using the time-hallowed phrases of Babylonian dedications, his restoration of Borsippa's main temple in perfect accord with long established Mesopotamian building rituals.[56]

---

54 Discussed by R. J. van der Spek, 'The Babylonian city' in A. Kuhrt and S. Sherwin-White, 1987 (above n. 10), 57–74 (67–8).

55 P. Briant, 1994 (above n. 48), 463–7.

56 Text, translation and discussion in A. Kuhrt and S. Sherwin-White, 'Aspects of royal Seleucid ideology. the cylinder of Antiochus I from Borsippa', *JHS*, 111 (1991), 71–86.

But, inserted into the middle of the sonorous recital of the traditional royal titles, his Macedonian descent is proudly and prominently advertised. This is a deviation from established Babylonian practice, where the king's ethnicity is not mentioned. Instead, as Pierre Briant has pointed out,[57] the formulation mirrors rather exactly the dedications made by hellenistic kings in Greek sanctuaries. Here, too, they call themselves not 'king of the Macedonians,' but *basileus Makedon*, i.e. 'the Macedonian king'. Pausanias, describing (6.3.1; 10.7.8) Ptolemaic dedications at Delphi and Olympia, refers to this practice and explains it: 'They called themselves 'Macedonian' although they were kings of Egypt, because they liked to be called so.' And in this purely Babylonian setting, too, Antiochus employs the epithet, thus reminding all that, while he may be a Babylonian king, he is simultaneously a Macedonian, member of the conquering group which now wields power. The emphasis on the ruler's ethnicity echoes the Achaemenid stress on the Persian identity and nature of their rule.

One other term makes its appearance in connection with Alexander's invasion and the early years of Seleucid rule in Babylonia. Alexander is characterized as coming from the land of Hana; his army is made up of 'Hanaeans'. If you cast your mind back to the first of the Mesopotamian world-maps I described (Figure 1b), you will recall that the far-off region beyond the 'Cedar Mountain' to the north-west is the land of Hana. The term had been transferred to this far-off country from its original, earlier location around the Middle Euphrates, where it defined a nomadic group — unruly trouble-makers who disrupted the peaceful tenor of civilized life. So, in the context of Mesopotamia's urban culture, they were barbarian outsiders, and by the first millennium, they are envisaged as continuing to live on, unchanged, on one of the far-off edges of the universe. In a seventh century text from Assurbanipal's library in Nineveh, they are further associated with the pillage about a thousand years earlier of the great cult-statue of Bel-Marduk, patron-god of Babylon, which had been recovered only in response to the piety of a Babylonian monarch.[58] Although the text comes from an Assyrian site and uses Assyrian scribal conventions, it is likely that the story was known in Babylonia, too, especially as it concerned the restitution of Babylon's chief cult, with which Assurbanipal himself was intimately concerned.[59] So it is with this negative stereotype of nomadic hordes, sacrilegious pillagers then, that Babylonian scholars appear to have identified the Graeco-Macedonian armies — although, interestingly, such an identification is not invariably, but selectively, applied.

---

57 P. Briant, 1994 (above n. 48), 461–3.

58 Discovery of text(s) and summary in T. Longman III, *Fictional Akkadian Autobiography: a generic and comparative study*, Winona Lake, IN, 1991, 83–6. Translation, *ibid*, 221–2.

59 For Assurbanipal's restoration work in Babylon, see J. Harmatta, 'Les modèles littéraires des l'édit babylonien de Cyrus', *Acta Iranica*, 1 (1974), 29–44.

To draw out the implications of the usage, we need to examine some more texts. When an astronomical diary, in 331, describes Alexander's first entry into Babylon, his pacific and pious overtures to the citizens are noted, and his forces are described as 'Ionian', and he is called, uniquely, 'king of the world'. This becomes 'king of countries', the title given to the Persian rulers in Babylonia, in the next year, while, in 329/8, the diary entry refers to him as 'the king who is from the land of Hani'.[60] Given the very fragmentary state of preservation of the diary texts, it is not easy to know exactly what to make of this, nor of a couple of other mentions, in very broken contexts, of Hana and Hanaean troops in 329/8 and 323/2.[61] But a pseudo-prophecy, almost certainly composed in the early years of Seleucid rule, gives us a clearer sense (Figure 6c.1).[62] In the passage cited, the 'prophet' predicts the murder of the Persian king Arses in 336, followed by a period of crisis and then Darius III's accession and reign. After five years of rule, in 331/0, a Hanaean army attacks and loots his realm. Following this setback, Darius III makes a successful comeback, repels the invaders and re-establishes calm and prosperity, marked by the granting of tax-exemptions. The anti-historical nature of the text has given rise to much discussion, and the precise interpretation is moot.[63] It seems to me best understood as a programmatic text, pointing to the ways in which Babylonian political support may best be mobilized, by presenting the period between Darius III's death and the beginnings of Seleucid rule as one of anarchy and chaos, with order re-established by the Seleucid régime.[64]

But however one understands it, what is indisputable is that Alexander's army is dubbed Hanaean in a context which makes it clear that it is the threatening, barbarian aura of the name, against which the forces of good might be victoriously mobilized, that is being played upon. Similarly, in the 'Chronicle of the Successors', we find Macedon as the home country of the legitimate, accepted king (Figure 6b.1). But, when the chronicle moves on to the year of Philip's assassination and Antigonus' devastating move into Babylonia, his forces are described as Hanaean.[65] The impression that grows upon the reader of these

60 A. J. Sachs and H. Hunger, 1988–96 (above n. 33), I: no. –330, rev. 9 and 11; no. –329, obv. B 1; no. –328, LE 1. For the suggestion that the last text indicates Babylonian hostility to Alexander, see P. Briant, 1996 (above n. 10), 883, 1076.

61 A. J. Sachs and H. Hunger, 1988–96 (above n. 33), I: no. –328, rev. 27; no. –322, D obv. 22.

62 Text published by A. K. Grayson, *Babylonian Historical-Literary Texts*, Toronto, 1975, 24–37.

63 D. J. Wiseman, 'Review of Grayson, 1975' (above n. 62), *BSOAS*. 40 (1977), 373–5. C. Mazzetti, 'Voina Dariya so Skifami i Vavilonskaya prorocheskaya literatura', *VDI*, 3 (1982), 106–10. G. Marasco, 'La "Profezia Dinastica" e la resistenza babilonese alla conquista di Alessandro', *ASNP*, 15/2 (1985), 529–38. M. J. Geller, 'Babylonian astronomical diaries and corrections of Diodorus', *BSOAS*, 53 (1990), 1–7.

64 H. Ringren, 'Akkadian apocalypses', in D. Hellholm, ed., *Apocalypticism in the Mediterranean World and the Near East,* (Proceedings of the International Colloquium on Apocalypticism, Uppsala, August 12–17, 1979), Tübingen, 1983, 379–86. S. Sherwin-White, 1987 (above n. 53), 10–14.

65 A. K. Grayson, *Assyrian and Babylonian Chronicles,* (Texts from Cuneiform Sources, 5), Locust Valley, N.Y., 1975, no. 10, obv. 17.

passages is that where the invading Greek-Macedonian armies appear in contexts that are not obviously pacific, the Babylonian writers choose to call them, perjoratively, 'Hanaean', i.e. 'barbarians from the north-western edge of the world'.[66] And the fact that we are not forcing the interpretation too much is borne out by two factors. First, the word is not applied to Greek-Macedonian forces, individuals or practices after the early years of Seleucid rule,[67] which suggests that it was only felt to be applicable to the appalling experiences of the time of turmoil, ushered in by Alexander and gradually reversed by Seleucus I. Secondly, in the eyes of the Babylonian chronicler, Seleucus I himself, his troops and country of origin do not belong to the category of 'Hanaeans'. When he describes Seleucus mustering his soldiers in 282, they seem to be called Ionian, and when he sets out from Sardis in 281, he crosses, as we saw, to 'Macedon, his country'(Figure 6b.2). But when the Babylonian compiler of a later king-list looks back after the middle of the second century B.C. to the vile murder of Seleucus, after his landing in Thrace, in 281, he describes it as happening in the land of the barbarous Hanaeans (Figure 6c.2).

## Conclusion

Looking at the politically dominant realms of the ancient world between the eighth and third centuries B.C., we can see that, despite political changes, there is a considerable consistency in the configuration of the earth as envisaged and publicly projected by their rulers. In this, Greeks occupy a marginal space: they remain a disparate, remote people living on the edge of the world. But when the established balance is upset, the kaleidoscope is shaken and the image becomes more complex, as the periphery becomes in some respects the centre — the outsiders become insiders. And in this context, the old ethnic 'Hanaean' is revived, to resonate with traditional ideas of the ordered cosmos threatened by chaotic forces. Where we can pin it down, 'Hanaean' seems to function in some respects analogously to the way that Germans were labelled 'Huns' at the time, and in the context of, the First World War.[68] Here, too, an archaic tag, with nebulous but fearsome connotations (which had actually nothing to do with Germany), was attached to a powerful aggressor, whose crude image, in the context of a horrific war, was that of a barbarian. But its appropriateness was, of

---

66 A point made by F. Joannès, 'Le monde occidental vu de Mésopotamie, de l'époque néo-babylonienne à l'époque hellénistique', *Transeuphratène*, 13 (1997), 141–53 (150), i.e. that it is not, as some have thought (e.g. J. -J. Glassner, *Chroniques Mésopotamiennes*, Paris, 1993, 53), a name for Macedon, in particular (nor Thrace, as suggested by A. L. Oppenheim in J. B. Pritchard, ed., *Ancient Near Eastern Texts relating to the Old Testament*, 2nd ed., Princeton, N.J., 1969, 567).

67 *Cf.* F. Joannès, 1997 (above n. 66), 150–1.

68 In the British context, 'Hun(s)' is first used in the sense of (members of) a reckless/barbaric horde in 1806, according to the *Oxford Concise Dictionary*, 3rd ed., Oxford, 1933, and then applied to characterize the German mode of warfare during World War I. (I owe this information to Carlotta Dionisotti.)

course, limited: as an armistice was declared, tensions defused, and political relations normalized, use of the term declined. Similarly, too, in the Babylonian milieu, the Hanaean label seems only to have been applicable to some Greek-Macedonian actors for a restricted period and in particularly violent situations, while care seems to have been taken to distance the Macedonian Seleucids themselves from any possible derogatory associations. Certainly, they hailed from the same wild and remote region of Hana, but they were also legitimately sanctioned Babylonian kings, and as such not to be confused with the 'barbarian Greeks'.

# CHRONOLOGICAL OUTLINE

**Neo-Assyrian Empire: 934–*c*.610**

Tiglath-pileser III (745–727)
Sargon II (722–705)
Sennacherib (705–681)
Esarhaddon (681–669)
Assurbanipal (669–631?)

**Neo-Babylonian Empire: 626–539**

Nebuchadnezzer II (605–562)
Nabonidus (556–539)

**Achaemenid Empire: 559–330**

Cyrus II 'the Great' (559–530)
Cambyses II (530–522)
Darius I (522–486)
Xerxes (486–465)
Darius III (336–330)

**Beginnings of Macedonian Rule in Babylonia: 331–260**

| | |
|---|---|
| 331–323: | Alexander III 'the Great' |
| 323–316: | Philip III Arrhidaeus (documents date by him for a year after his murder in 317) |
| 321/0–315: | Seleucus, satrap of Babylonia |
| 316/5: | Alexander IV |
| 315–311: | Antigonus 'the general' controls Babylonia |
| 312/1 | Seleucus returns to Babylon (retrospectively start of Seleucid Era) |
| 310–308: | Extensive fighting between Antigonus' forces and Seleucus 'the general' |
| 305: | Seleucus assumes kingship title |
| before 301: | Probable founding of Seleucia-Tigris |
| late 294: | Crown prince Antiochus appointed co-regent |
| 281: | Seleucus assassinated; accession of Antiochus I |
| 271: | Completion of restoration of Esagila temple in Babylon |
| 268: | Completion of rebuilding of the Ezida temple in Borsippa |
| 261: | Death of Antiochus I; accession of Antiochus II |

Figure 4 — Chronological Outline

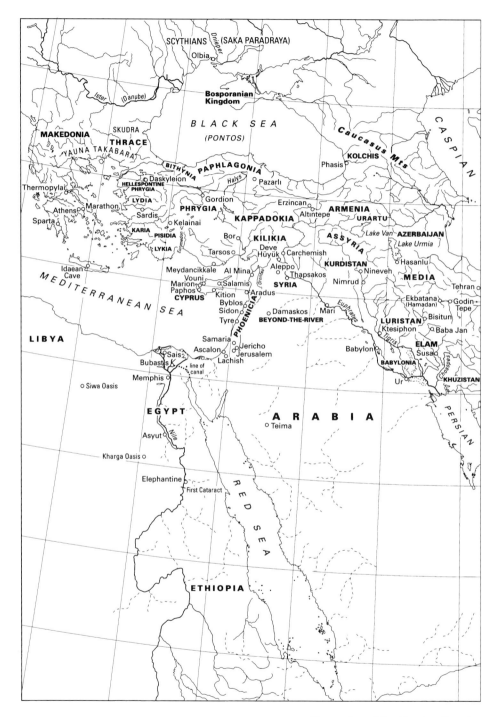

Figure 5 — The Persian Empire

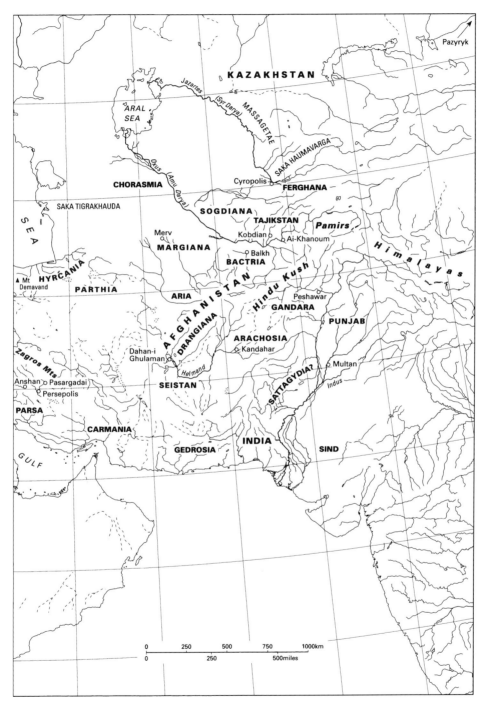

(after M. C. Miller, 1997)

# Greeks/Macedonians in Babylonian Hellenistic Texts

## a — *Ionia/Ionians*

1 – [ . . . ]there was famine in Babylonia; people sold their children. People died of xx. That year (274/3), there was *ekketu*-disease [ . . . ] Purchases in Babylon and the (other) cities were made with copper coins of Ionia.

(*AD, –273*)

2 – That month (August–September, 169), I heard as follows: King Antiochus entered victoriously into the cities of Egypt. The citizens (*pulite = politai*) [performed?] a procession (*puppe = pompe*) according to an Ionian pattern.,

(*AD, –168*),

3 – Year 30, Siwan (May–June, 282): that month, [Seleucus, the king,] mustered [his troops] and [marched] to the land [ . . . ]. The Ionians [ . . . ].

(*ABC, 12*)

## b — *Macedon/Macedonian*

1 – The fifth year of Philip (319/8): In an unknown month, the king [ . . . ] Antigon[us . . . Antipater] crossed to Macedon (*Makdunu*) and did not return [ . . .].

(*ABC, 10*)

2 – Year 3[1], [month] (281): [ . . . ] his [troops] fron Sar[dis], he mustered and took [across] the sea [ . . . ] with him, to Macedon (*Makkadunu*), his land [ . . . ].

(*ABC, 12*)

3 – Antiochus, the great king, the mighty/legitimate king, king of the world, king of Babylon, king of lands, caretaker of Esagila and Ezida, first/foremost son of Seleucus, the king, the Macedonian, king of Babylon, am I.

(F. H. Weissbach, *Die Keilinschriften der Achämeniden*,
(Vorderasiatische Bibliothek 3), Leipzig, 1911, 132–3.
A. Kuhrt and S. Sherwin-White, *JHS*, 111 (1991), 75–6)

## c — *Hana/Hanaeans*

1 – For two years [he will exercise kingship] (i.e. Arses = Artaxerxes IV, 338–6). A eunuch (i.e. Bagoas) [will murder] that king.

Any prince [will arise]. He will attack and [will seize the thron]e. He will [exercise kingship] for five years (i.e. Darius III, 336–330). [ . . . ] army of the Hanaeans [ . . . ] will attack [ . . . ]. His army [ . . . ] will plunder and ro[b him]. Afterwards, [his ar]my will regroup and raise their weapons. Enlil, Shamash and [Marduk] will go at the side of his ar[my]. He will bring about the overthrow of the Hanaean army. He will [carry] off his extensive booty [and bring] it into his palace. The people who had ex[perienced] misfortune [will enjoy] well-being. The mood of the land [ . . . ] tax exemption [ . . . ].

(*BHLT, 34–5*)

2 – Year 31, month VI (August–September, 281), Se[leucus] the king was killed in the land [of the] Hanaeans.

(A. J. Sachs and D. J. Wiseman, *Iraq*, 16 (1954), 203 and 205)

Figure 6 – Greeks/Macedonians in Babylonian Hellenistic Texts